127

little ways
you can make
a big difference
in the world

GUERRILLAS

Join the Goodness Revolution

OF GOODNESS

HANDBOOK

BY MOLLI NICKELL • ILLUSTRATED BY GARY LUND

(WORKMAN)

Library of Congress Cataloging-in-Publication Data
Nickell, Molli
Guerrillas of Goodness Handbook: 127 little ways you can
make a big difference in the world / by Molli Nickell
illustrations by Gary Lund.
p. cm.
ISBN 1-56305-561-9 (pbk.)
1. Kindness—Miscellanea.
2. Conduct of life—Miscellanea.
I. Lund, Gary   II. Title.
BJ1533. K5N53   1994   94-6241
177'.7—dc20   CIP

Workman Publishing Company, Inc.
708 Broadway
New York, NY 10003

First printing April 1994
Printed in Canada

10 9 8 7 6 5 4 3 2 1

—Hugs of Appreciation—

To the unsung heroes, the original Guerrillas of Goodness: Ann, Armond, Gina, Georgia, Glenn, Jamie, Karen, Lisa, Mary, Michelle, Myron, Sharon, and Susan—thank you!

To Bob Silverstein for his support, inspiration and outstanding literary representation—thank you! To Sally Kovalchick, whose focused stewardship and creative talent helped to crystallize this handbook—thank you!

And to the other unmentioned participants in this gentle revolution who believe that it is possible to create a more peaceful planet—thank you!

Molli Nickell
Gary Lund

A quiet revolution of a different nature is sweeping the planet. Thousands of people just like you are joining forces to make a big difference in the world. They are becoming Guerrillas of Goodness, performing thoughtful acts of goodness in an effort to improve others' lives.

Goodwin Gorilla, representing gentle beings who live in harmony with each other and with the planet, dances across the pages that follow, illustrating anonymous acts of goodness by individuals across the country. His name, "Goodwin," hints at the win-win opportunities that will come your way when you join their ranks.

You see, the most amazing thing happens when you spontaneously open your heart to help another. You feel happy. The recipient feels happy, loved and valued. It's absolutely contagious—viral goodness.

Recipients become Guerrillas of Goodness in turn, and the movement toward creation of a more peaceful planet spreads from person to person.

We invite you to join in the movement. Like pebbles tossed into a pond, we can, acting together, create gentle ripples to wash over the planet as we inspire others to become Guerrillas of Goodness and join us until we create a flood.

(Noah, you ain't seen nothing yet!)

1 A businessman in Cincinnati, Ohio, picks up litter that accumulates around the outside of his office building.

2 A Chicago secretary makes it a point to smile at everyone who gets on the elevator with her.

3 In Philadelphia, a philharmonic violinist puts on free concerts for children who no longer have music programs in their schools.

4 In Pontiac, Michigan, a man who's retired gives himself weekly doses of laughter by renting a funny video and sharing it with friends.

acts of
goodness
you can
do for
yourself

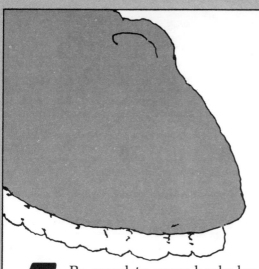

5 Be good to your body by eating a piece of fruit, instead of candy, as your midafternoon snack.

6 Every time you look at yourself in the mirror, smile!

7 Treat yourself to a long nap in the middle of the day.

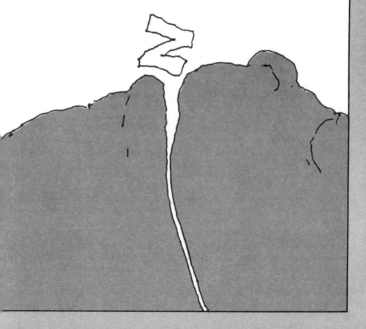

8 Take a "well" day off from work and enjoy a movie.

9 Release tension as you fly a kite on a windswept hill.

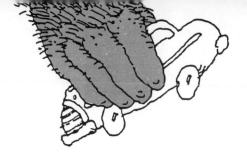

10 In Wilmington, Delaware, a man buys a new car and gives his old one to a family in need of transportation.

11 A man in Little Rock, Arkansas, offers a ride to a senior citizen struggling with heavy grocery bags.

12 A family of five spends Christmas Day pitching in at a nearby soup kitchen in Dallas, Texas.

13 In Portland, Oregon, teenage volunteers sweep floors and wash windows in a run-down shelter for the homeless.

14 A grandmother in Cheyenne, Wyoming, spends her Christmas gift money on McDonald's certificates that she distributes to homeless people.

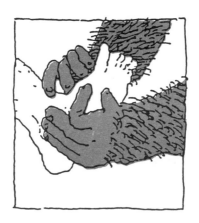

15 A massage practitioner gives free foot rubs to residents at a senior citizens' home in Seattle, Washington.

16 After the riots in Los Angeles, California, thousands of people show up to help clean the streets.

17 A New York City cabbie waves pedestrians through a gridlocked intersection.

18 In Hollywood, California, a movie producer flies his mother to town for shopping and a special lunch on Mother's Day.

acts of
goodness
you can
do for
your parents

19 Call them, ask about their lives and *really* listen to them.

20 Share special childhood memories with them.

21 Send them on an all-expenses-paid vacation.

22 Hug them as often as possible.

23 A businessman forgives a debt to help an associate restructure and revitalize his business in St. Louis, Missouri.

24 A woman driver pays the toll on a turnpike in Indianapolis, Indiana—and also pays for the three cars behind her.

25 In Castlerock, Maine, a woman inspires co-workers to be spontaneous as she skips down a long hall to the copyroom.

26 At their annual block party in San Bruno, California, residents help each other plant trees and paint mailboxes to beautify their neighborhood.

27 In Detroit, Michigan, a woman drops off hot homemade meals in the poorest section of town.

28 Children in Topeka, Kansas, sell baked goods at their school to raise money for food and books for children in Somalia.

acts of goodness you can do for those in other countries

29 Become a pen pal with an adult or child in a foreign country.

30 Send lifesavers and magazines to U.S. servicemen stationed abroad (a project sponsored by the American Red Cross).

31 Give financial aid to (adopt) a child.

32 A teenager in Des Moines, Iowa, cleans snow off her driveway, then does the same for the neighbors.

33 A girl scout troop in Knoxville, Tennessee, collects canned goods and delivers them to those living in a shelter.

34 In Omaha, Nebraska, high school students produce puppet shows for kindergarteners in the inner city.

acts of goodness you can do for those in the inner city

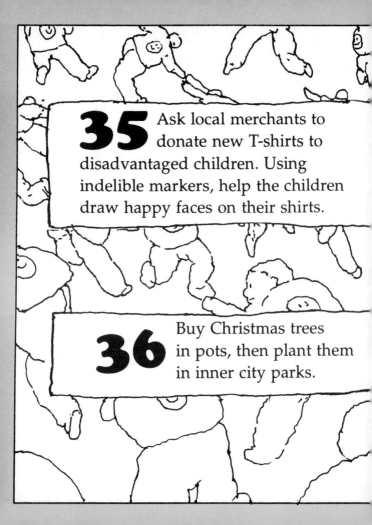

35 Ask local merchants to donate new T-shirts to disadvantaged children. Using indelible markers, help the children draw happy faces on their shirts.

36 Buy Christmas trees in pots, then plant them in inner city parks.

37 Lead sing-alongs with children at your local grammar school.

38 Repaint grafitti-covered walls with rainbows.

39 Read stories to first-graders.

40 Donate your used books to an inner-city library.

41 Collect and repair sports equipment, then give it to an inner-city athletic program.

42 Farmers in Kansas send hay to feed farm animals in a drought-stricken area of Georgia. The next year, Georgia farmers send peaches to their benefactors in Kansas.

43 At Kennedy Airport
in New York City,
a woman helps a physically
challenged man by carrying
his suitcase from the airport
exit to the taxi stand.

44 A veteran beachcomber cleans up trash as she walks along the beaches of Cape Cod, Massachusetts.

45 Distributors across the country ship books, at no charge, to restock a burned-out bookstore in Biloxi, Mississippi, so it can reopen for business.

46 A woman in Silver Springs, Maryland, brings nourishing homemade soup to those in the hospital.

acts of
goodness
you can do
for those
who are ill

47 Give them a soft robe or bed jacket.

48 Read to them.

49 Knit colorful lap blankets for them.

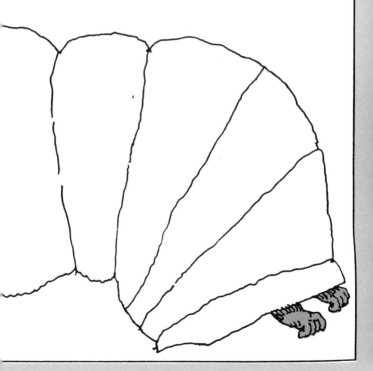

50 A teacher in Scranton, Pennsylvania, enlists the cooperation of other teachers to start a college savings account for a promising student from an economically challenged family.

51 A radio DJ in Bisbee, Arizona, helps raise money to replace athletic track construction funds stolen from a local grammar school.

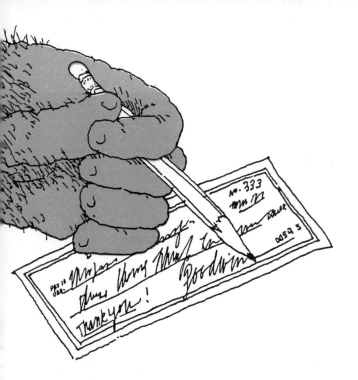

52 In Salt Lake City, Utah, a secretary writes "Thank You" on his checks.

53 A woman from Kenosha, Wisconsin, on a transoceanic flight, gives up her aisle seat to a long-legged fellow traveler.

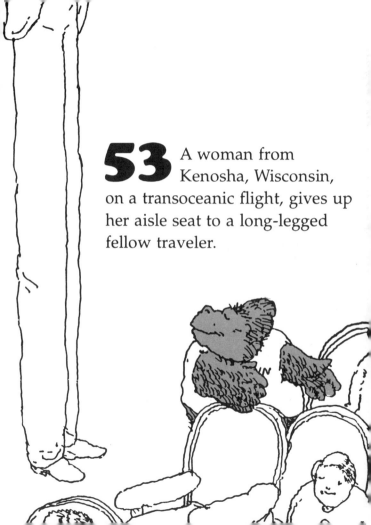

54 In Miami, Florida, high school baseball players donate weekend coaching sessions to a nearby grammar school whose athletic program has been cut due to lack of funds.

55 In Fresno, California, a college student collects recyclables and gives them to homeless people so they can redeem them.

56 A secretary in Twin Falls, Idaho, gives a box of donuts to the mechanics who repaired her car.

57

A couple in Lexington, Kentucky, packs out trash when hiking in the woods.

acts of
goodness
you can
do for
wilderness
areas

58 Move rocks aside to smooth out hiking trails.

59 Leave campsites cleaner than you found them.

60 Create a supply of firewood in areas containing fire pits.

61 A homeless man in Pasadena, California, tackles a thief to retrieve the purse of a British tourist.

62 During a hot spell in Erie, Pennsylvania, a family invites neighbors to cool off in the backyard.

63 On Valentine's Day, a retired pensioner in Tucson, Arizona, buys a sheet cake decorated with hearts and serves it to everyone he meets in the park.

64 A healing professional in Bremerton, Washington, urges her audience to practice gentle kindness to those recovering from mental illness.

65 A businessman in Denver, Colorado, adopts a stray cat he found scavenging outside his office complex.

acts of
goodness
you can
do for
animals

66 Borrow puppies and kittens from the animal shelter to take on a visit to a senior citizens' center.

67 Find a home for a pet—and have it neutered beforehand.

68 Send doggie bones and chewy toys to animals awaiting adoption at the shelter.

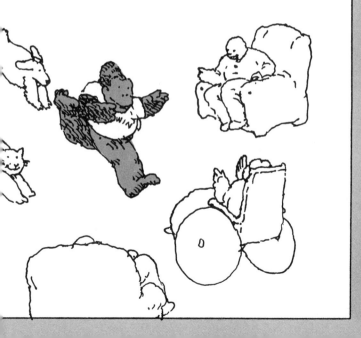

69 Hang popcorn strings on the trees to feed winter birds.

70 Make natural habitats such as straw piles for rabbits or watering holes for other wild animals in your area.

71 Instead of killing them, capture intrusive animals and transport them to the wild.

72 In Visalia, California, a shopper gives the clerk an extra $20 to pay for groceries of the senior citizen in line behind him.

73 After the Los Angeles earthquake, a woman whose home was undamaged donates blankets and dishes to those whose homes were destroyed.

74 An art dealer in Washington, D.C., lends paintings to a local school to encourage art appreciation.

75 The members of a household in Burbank, California, prepare food and gifts for a family they sponsor at Christmas time.

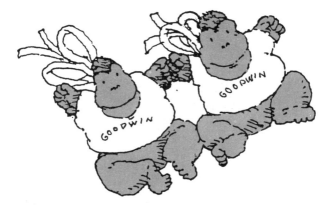

76 In Seattle, Washington, a homemaker, when buying gifts for any occasion, purchases an extra gift for donating to a needy family.

77 A 10-year-old girl in Tucson, Arizona, collects colorful desert rocks, then sells them and donates the proceeds to homeless people.

78 In Eugene, Oregon, neighbors pitch in to harvest fall crops for a neighbor who is physically disabled.

79 A grammar school teacher collects clothing, then washes, presses and delivers it to a halfway house for battered women and their children in Tulsa, Oklahoma.

80 In Baltimore, Maryland, seniors volunteer to hold and rock AIDS and drug-affected babies at a community hospital.

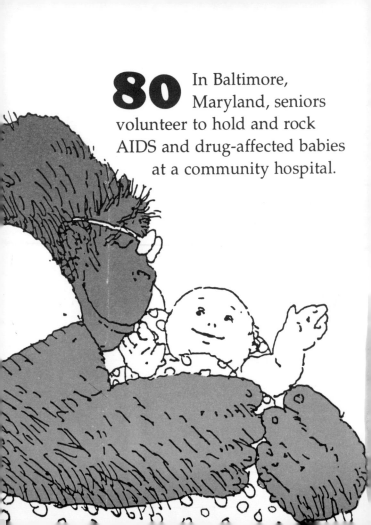

acts of goodness you can do for people with AIDS

81 Bake an extra casserole and donate it to your local hospice.

84

82 Send notes or flowers to those who are bedridden to let them know you're thinking about them.

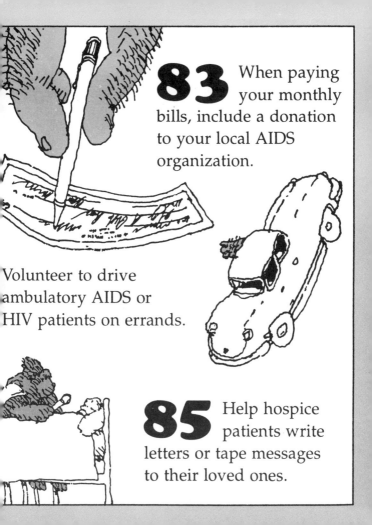

83 When paying your monthly bills, include a donation to your local AIDS organization.

84 Volunteer to drive ambulatory AIDS or HIV patients on errands.

85 Help hospice patients write letters or tape messages to their loved ones.

86 A retired woman in Winter Haven, Florida, operates a "friend in need" hot line for people who feel they have to talk to someone.

87 A hairdresser in Mobile, Alabama, gives haircuts and shampoos to shut-ins.

88 In Honolulu, Hawaii, a woman takes pictures of her children being playfully silly and sends them to her in-laws.

acts of
goodness
you can
do for
your in-laws

89 The next time you see your mother-in-law, give her a big hug.

90 Spend a day with your sister-in-law.

91 Forgive your in-laws for any transgressions (supposed or real).

92 Forgive yourself for having judged them. Love yourself and them—warts and all.

93

Send your mother-in-law a postcard with a joke on it.

94

Frame your children's paintings and send them to both grandmothers.

95 A retired civil engineer donates one day a week to complete bulk mailings for a nonprofit organization in Brentwood, California.

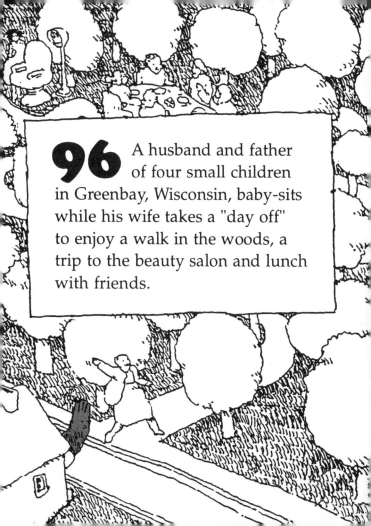

96 A husband and father of four small children in Greenbay, Wisconsin, baby-sits while his wife takes a "day off" to enjoy a walk in the woods, a trip to the beauty salon and lunch with friends.

97 A teenager in Missoula, Montana, keeps his elderly neighbor supplied with firewood all winter.

98 A commuter in Joplin, Missouri, gives his spare to a nurse who is stranded on the freeway with a flat and no extra tire.

99 A woman in Atlanta, Georgia, places radiantly blooming potted plants on the doorsteps of skid row hotels.

100 A man refills the parking meter for the next car as he leaves his space in Wichita, Kansas.

101 In Santa Clara, California, residents transform a barren strip of freeway island by tossing wildflower seeds into the dirt during the rainy season.

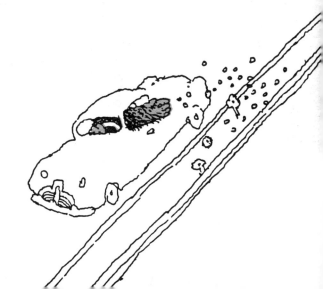

102 A woman in Rockford, Illinois, takes small gifts of appreciation to her dentist.

acts of
goodness
you can
do for
health care
givers

103 Send them a gift certificate to your favorite restaurant.

104 Give them a jar of your homemade preserves (or sugarless cookies).

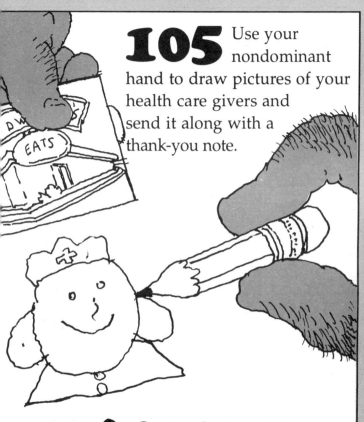

105 Use your nondominant hand to draw pictures of your health care givers and send it along with a thank-you note.

106 Create a basket of finger foods (from apples to mint truffles) for the entire office staff to share.

107 A mother gives a bright bouquet to a school-crossing guard who's always on the job—rain, snow or shine—in Fargo, North Dakota.

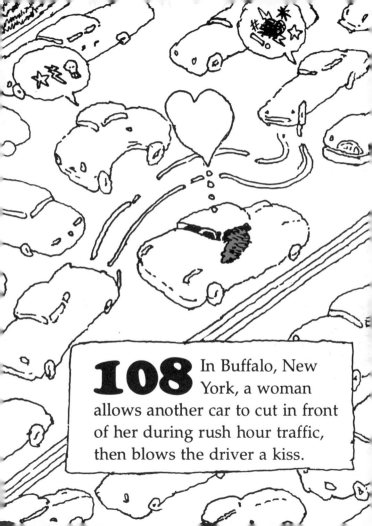

108 In Buffalo, New York, a woman allows another car to cut in front of her during rush hour traffic, then blows the driver a kiss.

110 A teenager in Twin Falls, Idaho, gives a magazine subscription to a house-bound neighbor.

111 A Portland, Oregon, advertising executive gives her secretary a box of candy as thanks for her assistance during a hectic week.

112 In Austin, Texas, a retired Country Western star invites 22 homeless people to join her for Christmas dinner and caroling.

113 During the floods in Des Moines, Iowa, farmers with inundated fields gather in prayer vigils to ask that farmlands downstream be spared.

114

Conservationists band together and recycle Christmas trees into brush fences to contain and improve the wetlands' silt level in Baton Rouge, Louisiana.

acts of
goodness
you can
do for
Mother
Earth

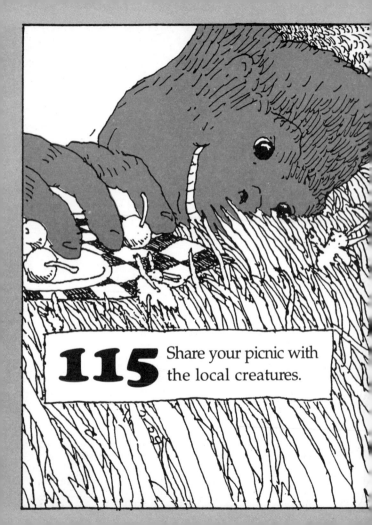

115 Share your picnic with the local creatures.

116 Rather than swatting at them, allow bees to perform their service of pollination.

117 Use a brown paper bag to save newspapers for recycling.

118 Dance with gratitude as you thank Mother Earth for her generous hospitality.

119 Throw away at least one aerosol can.

120 Bike or walk, instead of driving, on short trips.

121 After a successful paper drive, a room mother in Redding, California, bakes a celebratory cake for the children.

122 An office worker in Manhattan, New York, leaves encouraging notes on the desks of her co-workers.

123 A printer in Pontiac, Michigan, donates 100 bumper stickers to a junior high school student to distribute to her classmates.

acts of
goodness
you can do
to spread the
word about
goodness

124 Encourage grammar school students to create and then donate colorful bookmarks to the library.

125 Order address labels and place them on all your envelopes.

A gentle planet begins with gentle people.

Become a Guerrilla of Goodness.

126 Organize a group to paint inspirational murals on the walls of the cafeteria at a local high school.

127 Enlist Guerrillas of Goodness by sharing this handbook and its philosophy with others.

There must be several gadzillion other simple and loving acts you can do for others. It doesn't take much effort. Be spontaneous. The less planning, the better.

And be anonymous. Let Goodwin Gorilla take all the credit. At the site of each act of goodness, leave behind one of the "Guerrilla of Goodness" stickers tucked inside this book. Each little reminder that someone cares just might encourage others to perform similar acts of kindness.

See how it goes? Person to person. That's how all revolutions begin and continue—with individual acts.

May the next one be yours.

Become a Guerrilla of Goodness

Author Molli Nickell and illustrator Gary Lund have worked together as a team since 1984, when they co-founded *Spirit Speaks* magazine, a "reader's digest" of spiritual psychology.

Molli—a syndicated columnist, motivational speaker and seminar leader—and her husband Glenn live on a 30-acre retreat and guest ranch in Tucson, Arizona.

Artist Gary Lund, whose designs have graced dozens of book and magazine covers since 1965, resides in Santa Fe, New Mexico. He has won an Emmy and also has been nominated for an Academy Award for his work in animation.

If you would like to receive a complimentary *Spirit Speaks* sampler magazine, call toll-free, 1-800-356-9104, or write to Molli Nickell at Paz Entera Ranch, P.O. Box 85400, Tucson, AZ 85754.

Some of the proceeds from this book support The Gorilla Foundation and Koko—a mountain gorilla who has learned to communicate with humans using American Sign Language. For information on the foundation and their programs, write The Gorilla Foundation, Box 620-530, Woodside, CA 94062.